You Are
Special

[-adj, exceptional; surpassing what
is common or usual; designed or
reserved for a particular purpose;
unique; remarkable; extraordinary]

[-n, Precious; a dearly beloved person]

© 2011 Nancy Goudie

ISBN 978-1-907636-08-0

Edited by Ray Goudie

Design of this episode by Nancy Goudie, Ray Goudie and Peter C. Series design by Helen Martin.

Cover and interior illustrations by Charlotte Cooke

Published by New Generation Music. Caedmon Complex, Bristol Road, Thornbury, Bristol, BS35 3JA, UK. www.ngm.org.uk

Print management by Verité. 8 St John's Parade, Alinora Crescent, Goring-by-Sea, West Sussex, BN12 4HJ, UK.

Unless otherwise stated biblical quotations are taken from The Holy Bible, New International Version, Copyright © 1973, 1978, 1984 International Bible Society, used by permission of Zondervan Bible Publishers.

Scripture quotations marked 'The Message' are taken from The Message. Copyright 1993, 1994, 1995. Used by permission of NavPress Publishing Group

Preface

This is my third and final book in this series. Each book has been designed in such a way that you can open it at any page and feel encouraged and uplifted. Like the others in the series, this book is full of real stories, wise words, meditations, love songs, quotes and prophetic words, which are all crafted in a way that shows you how incredibly special you are.

In our culture of stress, with so much pressure to look good and be famous, we often need to be reminded just how unique, precious, remarkable and extraordinary we are! No matter which country we were born in, what colour our skin is, what size we are, what intelligence we display, what background we come from, the truth is each one of us is an exceptional human being. In every page of this book you will discover the truth about yourself and realise afresh that you are deeply loved, special and accepted. There is hope and huge encouragement painted on each page. So pick up this book at any time, open it at any page and discover afresh that...

you are special.

[Special]

is a word used to describe a one of a kind like a kiss, a sunset, a snowflake....

YOU!

Special applies to something or someone who is admired, precious, unique and cannot ever be replaced. Special best describes

YOU!

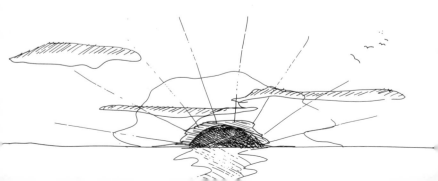

Believing you are Special

"Nancy, you're my closest friend –
not Ray, not anyone else – but you!!"

Throughout the latter part of my teenage years, I met and became instant friends with a girl called Sheila. She and I went everywhere together – we had lots of fun and still remain close friends to this day even though she lives in the States and I live in the UK. When I was a child, I remember quite vividly being told by someone who was annoyed with me that no-one would ever want to be my friend. Although I knew the person who had said those words didn't mean them, the impact of them remained with me and at times haunted me.

I met and married a man who is a very friendly, likeable guy and in my mind I could understand why people would like him more than me. The words spoken over me kept coming into my mind and at times, they caused me to question why anyone would ever like me or really want to be my friend.

One day whilst talking to Sheila, I was shocked to discover that she saw me as her special friend. She explained that although she liked Ray, my husband and saw him as a good friend, she saw me as her close friend and she regarded our friendship as extra special. It was a real revelation to me and brought so much healing to my life.

So if you are anything like me, then my prayer is that this little book will reveal to you that you are extra special and knowing that truth will bring so much healing and wholeness to your life.

You are Special

Believing you are special is difficult for most of us. We often need reminding that there is no-one quite like us. If you are anything like me, it will be easy to think negative thoughts about yourself and perhaps even about your body; wishing you were different, more likeable, more shapely. I want to take you on a journey that will help you see that you have been sculpted and formed by kind, gentle and loving hands and that in all the world there is no-one quite like you.

Take a couple of deep breaths, breathing in through your nose and out through your mouth. Then speak to your soul and say, "Listen soul, listen to the voice of truth." Now close your eyes and come with me on a journey of truth.

Now begin to use your imagination to see a man sitting in a workshop, working with a piece of clay. You look at the clay and wonder if he could make any beautiful thing from something that looks so ugly. You watch as he gently, but firmly moulds the clay and as you do, you realise this is a master craftsman at work. You watch his large hands craft the most delicate of pots, each detail is completed with expert skill. It does not seem to matter how long this creation takes to make, as long as when he is finished, he rejoices in it. You notice that as each lump of clay gradually disappears, what takes shape before your eyes is an amazing sculpture. He lovingly shapes his creation; he takes time over fine details to make sure everything is perfect. You realise that this potter does not make any mistakes, he does not make something and then discard it, but he rejoices in what he is making and is delighted with each of his creations. Each one is different and yet so special. As you watch, listen to the voice of truth within you. Truth speaks to you and says, "Just as this potter moulded and crafted this piece of clay, so did I mould you in your mother's womb. You are not a mistake, but gentle, loving hands created you. Just as each of this potter's creations are special, so are you special."

As you begin to leave your meditation, say to yourself several times, "I am special. There is no-one like me. I was shaped, formed and crafted in my mother's womb. I am wonderfully made. What a creation!"

Any time you feel ugly, unloved or negative about yourself, remember the potter. Go to a mirror and repeat the words, "I am special, there is no-one like me." Train yourself to say these words many times, because unless you are able to love and accept yourself, you cannot fully love others.

(c) Nancy Goudie. Meditation
on Peace like a river CD

Love is...

Tender Compassionate

Strong

Selfless

Sacrificial

Without limits

To be shared

Without conditions

Joy Peace

An action

Not controlling

Laying down your life

Giving without expecting

Passion Unity

True Unstoppable

Faithful

Compelling Inviting Pure

Merciful

Ceaseless

Humble

...GOD

Torn in Two

"My heart feels like it's being torn out of my body when you leave the room."

This was a comment from my son, Aidan when he was a young child and I was about to leave his bedroom after putting him to bed. There was so much love, longing and intense feelings poured into those words; they touched my heart and made me never want to leave him!

Aidan's passionate words spoke volumes to me about the love and intense longing God has for us. Always remember, the truth is that every time you turn your back on God and walk out of his 'room', his heart is torn in two! He longs to hold you close to his heart and carry you, his wonderful child, in his arms!

Isaiah 40:11

Listen and you will hear a voice from above tell you how much he passionately loves you!

You Lift my Head

For years I've held my head in shame
No answer to my endless pain
I walk this desert desolate
I'm barren, empty, desperate.

They say I'm drunk on red, red wine
Its sorrow from a different vine
These tears I've cried, the times I've died
So many prayers I've sighed.

Everytime I hear a voice from Heaven say
My child you're beautiful
You gently wipe my falling tears away
When I feel you lift my head, I start to smile
Your peace like raindrops fall
Even though its taken me a while
Father please take my dreams, my all.

Your breath of life has breathed on me
You've changed my life amazingly
My barrenness, now fertile land
A priceless gift from your own hand.

I feel alive inside of me
Your love has made my life complete
I won't withhold your precious gift
I lay it at your feet.

Come to the Feast

"My precious one, I have loved you with an everlasting love. I have wrapped my arms around you and have covered you with my grace.

From before time began, I chose you and picked you out to be mine. I want to show you how much you are loved. I want you to know how much you are loved. Let me wrap my arms around you and let me take you to a new level in me.

Let me bring you to my feast, my huge, abundant and extravagant feast which I have prepared for you! Don't hang around with the dogs under the table only getting the crumbs of what I want to give you. Come, for I have much to show you; much to give you. Come and wash in the waterfall of my Spirit. Come and sit at your rightful place and enjoy the fresh banquet I have for you each and every day!"

Ps 36:7-8

How priceless is your unfailing love! Both high and low among men find refuge in the shadow of your wings. They feast on the abundance of your house; you give them drink from your river of delights.

Friends

God calls you... *Friend*

"I have called you friends, for everything that I learned from my Father I have made known to you!"

John 15:15

A friend is defined by being someone who knows everything about you and still totally accepts you as you are!

There is a friend who sticks closer than a brother

Prov 18:24

A friend hears the song in
my heart and sings it to me
when my memory fails.

Anonymous

7 reasons why you are special

You were chosen before the creation of the world

You are loved completely and unconditionally

You are unique, one of a kind. There is no-one exactly like you

You were given a precious gift - the gift of LIFE

You were fashioned in the womb by kind and loving hands

Someone gave their life so that you might live

You are never forsaken nor forgotten

I'M GLAD I'M ME

One day as my husband and I were chatting, he said to me "I'm glad that I'm me! I don't want to be Billy Graham. I don't want to be Andrew Lloydd Webber. I don't want to be anyone else but me! I love being me! I love the creativity that God has given me and I'm glad God made me, me!"

There are many who cannot say what my husband said that day! There are many who earnestly desire to be someone else. We look at others around us and wish we had been born with their beauty, creativity, talent, gifting, finance etc. We think their life must be so much better than ours. What we have missed is the beauty within and how much our life is worth. What we have missed is how much we are valued and loved. Each one of us has been chosen and each one wonderfully made. God looks at you and says,

Song of Songs 4:7
The Message

"You are beautiful from head to toe; absolutely flawless!"

He wraps his love around you and clothes you with his joy. You are special; a joy to behold. When you begin to believe these truths, then you can say with enormous truth and conviction

I'm glad I'm me!

The Bond of Love

Just after Ray and I got married we bought a dog and called him Dylan. He was named after the singer with the same name! He was an amazing dog and became a great companion to me when my husband had to travel away from home for three weeks of every month. Years later when we left Scotland and knew that unfortunately we could not take a dog with us, we found him a good home. It was with real and deep sadness that we had to leave him behind, but we never ever forgot Dylan and he never forgot us either. The bond of love was very strong! When we used to go back to Scotland on occasional visits, we went to see our four legged friend and he immediately knew it was us. We both received lots of licks and his excited barking told us that he was pleased to see us. Even though I am sure he never understood why we had to leave him behind, he knew he was special to us and we knew we were special to him. When you realise you are loved, you know you are special.

Know you are loved...

Know you are special

I'm your man!

Some years ago, I heard a lady tell a story of how she heard God speak to her through the story of Pride and Prejudice. She had just been to see the film and was thinking through what she saw and how amazing Mr. Darcy's love was for Elizabeth Bennet. She thought to herself, "Mr. Darcy looked at Elizabeth with such intensity, with such a deep and wonderful love. If anyone looked at me like that, I would love him forever." Immediately God spoke to her heart and said, "I'm your man! I look at you like that every day!"

Never forget how amazing, how intense, how loving, how unique, how faithful, how special, how beautiful is the love of God for each one of us! He looks at you today with such intense longing!

*Never was a mother so blind
to the faults of her child as
the Lord is towards us*

Daniel Considine 1930

Unconditional Love

I heard recently about a story of a dog that was flung out of a car which was driving at full speed along a road. The car sped on as the dog hit the concrete and ended up in the ditch. The occupants of the car obviously didn't care much for the dog, nor did they seem to value the dog's life. Despite the fact that the dog was bleeding badly, he got back up on his feet and started to run as best he could after the car and the owner who had mistreated him. His love and faithfulness did not fade even after being cruelly abused! His unconditional love was fully displayed.

This shows us a little of what God's love is like towards us. No matter how badly we treat God, no matter how many times we turn our backs on him, no matter how many times we ignore him, it does not change the fact that God loves us unconditionally! He still wants to be with us and be our friend.

Romans 5:8

But God demonstrates his own love for us in this: while we were still sinners, Christ died for us!

Surrounded by Love

I heard a story of a young boy, whose parents told him they were going to put him into a children's home when they realised he had been stealing! They were only trying to frighten him in order for his stealing to cease, but what it did was to cause him to have a deep sense of insecurity and fear that lasted for many years.

I heard another story of a young child who at the age of six heard his mum tell his dad that she wanted the dad to march his sibling down to the police station and ask the police to lock him up and leave him there because he had behaved so badly. The father did just that and marched the older brother who was almost eight out of the house. The younger brother sat on the windowsill hoping against hope that his brother would return. Half an hour passed and then he saw his father walking up the street on his own. The fear of abandonment and rejection gripped his heart and tears flooded down his face! Not only was he now alone, but he was sure he would be next! As he looked through the tears, he suddenly saw his brother about 30 yards behind his dad. Only then did the fear and terror begin to subside but again it took a long time before the effect of what happened was totally out of his system.

I am sure in both of these stories, the parents would not dream that their words and actions could cause such overwhelming fear and I am sure had they known they would have rectified the situation and spoken out their love and acceptance. However, many people do come from families where they are constantly put down and not loved and accepted for who they are. I heard a story of a grandmother who constantly picked on her grand-daughter. She could not see anything good in her at all and even at the age of five she would verbally abuse her and cause her deep rejection. When the little girl fell into a pond, instead of being hugged and comforted, her grandmother scolded her, made her have a cold bath and sent her to bed in her wet clothes.

When our family or friends reject us and cause us pain, remember that there is a friend who will never push us away, will always love us and think of us as special no matter what we have done! Instead of being gripped by fear we can know what it's like to be surrounded by love!

Perfect love casts out all fear

1 John 4:18

I Feel Like a Woman Again

In January 2010 I held my Spiritual Health Weekend in Preston and it was there that I met a lady who subsequently wrote to me to tell me her story.

She had gone through a year of matrimonial troubles and two court cases, one on the Thursday and one on the Friday before the conference started, neither of which went well. In 2009 her husband left her for another woman and now he wanted to take the children from her.

She wrote and told me that she arrived at the conference a broken woman, begging God to show her if he really exists. What happened was just incredible! In the first session God told her of his love for her and whispered in her ear, "You are my wife!"

On the Saturday afternoon each delegate receives a 'word from God' from me. I personally pray for each woman by name before the conference and ask God for an encouraging word for them. When she received her 'word' she was blown away by what was written on the card. Among other encouraging comments written on the card was a phrase from God which said, "I am your husband."

Later on before dinner she prayed with a totally un-known lady from the conference who told her that God loved her so much and that He had told her to give her a ring and placed it on her wedding finger! She left the conference fully knowing that she was loved and she told me in her letter

"Nancy, I feel like a woman again!"

The Dark Night

Have you ever discovered that in the middle of the night, whatever fears and concerns you have seem so much bigger? When my husband was ill from burnout and mostly everything went wrong in our lives (read my book 'Treasures of Darkness' for the full story), I often woke up in the middle of the night with a horrible gnawing sensation in the pit of my stomach. For a couple of seconds I could not remember why I felt as I did and then it would all flood back. Was Ray ever going to get well? Was he ever going to be able to go back to work? Was our family life ever going to be happy again? Would I once more hear laughter in our home? Would we be able to survive the difficulties and problems we were encountering? Fears and worries flooded my mind and soon I was consumed by them. My battle in the night became so strong at times that literally I would shake with fear. Then I would remember that God's word says I am special and that he can bring good out of every situation. In the night as I spoke out these truths I felt the fear and the worry begin to disappear. Our home situation was the same but I knew I was not alone – I had a powerful God to help me!

Ps30:5b

**Weeping may remain for a night,
but joy comes in the morning**

You've Forgotten Something!

We had a huge bill to pay before the end of the month! Where were we going to get the money from? Deadlines were creeping ever closer and no solution was in sight. Rather than do what so many in our society would do and go to the bank for a loan, we went to God in prayer. It was during those times of prayer that we heard God speak to us and tell us that he was going to expand our finances similar to the way he expanded the five loaves and two fish in the feeding of the 5,000 in Mark 6. I have always thought that story is amazing where someone's lunch was expanded to feed approximately 20,000 people! (The Bible documents that there were 5,000 men, but of course we know there were women and children too! Potentially there could have been anything up to 20,000 people). Throughout the weeks before the bill needed to be paid, we prayed many times thanking God for expanding our finances and for the miracle he was going to do. Somehow, and we don't exactly know how it happened, that is precisely what took place. When we got to the end of the month, we just had enough to pay the bill. I then turned to Ray and said, "This is great, but you know the bigger miracle will be how we are going to survive throughout this month." We had paid the bill, but it had taken everything we had to live on. Without something happening we would have no money for food, for bills, for my dad's 90th birthday and of course because it was December we would have no money for Christmas presents for our two boys.

Once more we turned to God in prayer and again God spoke to us and said, **"You've forgotten something!"**

At first, we could not understand what he meant.

"What have we forgotten Lord?" we asked.

The Lord explained, "You have forgotten the 12 basketfuls which were left over. I'm going to give you the same!" And that is what happened. Little by little, day by day, week by week, God supplied money for us to pay each bill, to feed our family, to pay for my dad's present and our part in his birthday celebrations and enough money for Christmas as well. In fact, at the end of December we even had money left over!

When you have financial difficulties and problems, don't immediately panic, but pray to God and wait for his instructions. Remember he sees us as his special children.

He is Jehovah Jireh our Provider

Sounds of Heaven

I had just finished my Spiritual Health Weekend in Bristol and although so many good things had happened during that time, I realised that I had made two small errors whilst speaking from the platform. It was those two errors that woke me up in the middle of the night! Even though I was not overly concerned about them during the day, in the night they became mountains. I began to worry about them and even though I tried to put them out of my mind and go back to sleep, I couldn't for they seemed to have taken a life of their own and they were haunting me. Eventually, I prayed and cried out to God saying, "I cannot stand this condemnation any longer Lord, help me to hear the sounds of Heaven." Immediately, I began to hear the noise of a wonderful joyful party! The Lord said to me, "Nancy we are rejoicing because of all the lives that have been changed at your Spiritual Health Weekend." Immediately, I smiled, relaxed and fell asleep. What was the point of worrying when Heaven was rejoicing!

Let's listen to the sounds of Heaven resounding in our ears

"Are not two sparrows sold for a penny?
Yet not one of them will fall to the ground
apart from the will of your Father. And
even the very hairs of your head are all
numbered. So don't be afraid; you are
worth more than many sparrows!"
Jesus

Matthew 10:29-31

Unique, beautiful, special – YOU!

I am writing this book on the edge of a lake. Across the lake stand some old yet very stunning trees and my eyes are constantly drawn to explore their beautiful shape. There are tall trees which seem to reach to the sky and yet there are others that are really small. Some are thick with green leaves and others are very bare. Some have branches that are cut off and others have branches that reach high and wide. Each tree is different and yet each one is bursting with creativity, beauty and grace! I am stunned at how special they all are. As I am exploring them with my eyes, God speaks to me and says, "Just as each one of these trees is different and portrays a different aspect of beauty, so does each human being!" We are all a different shape, colour, size and personality and yet each of us is beautiful and so very special. No individual should be compared to another; everyone is unique!

Never forget how unique, beautiful and special you are!

The favour of God is on you!
You do not need to strive to
receive it, you already have it!

ENJOY HIS FAVOUR TODAY
AND ALWAYS

I AM BLESSED

Luke 1:46-49

"My soul glorifies the Lord and my spirit rejoices in God my Saviour for he has been mindful of the humble state of his servant. From now on, all generations will call me blessed, for the Mighty One has done great things for me – holy is his name!"

Mary said "I am blessed" even though she knew that in a short while many would question her honesty and her sanity! An angel had spoken to Mary and told her that despite the fact she was a virgin, she would become pregnant and give birth to the Son of God. Even though she could not understand how this could possibly happen she said to the angel, "May it be to me as you have said!" Can you imagine how she broke the news to her family and friends? "An angel has spoken to me! I am pregnant but please believe me when I tell you that it was not a man who made me pregnant but it was the Holy Spirit!" How would these statements appear to Mary's mum and dad and how would it appear to Joseph, her fiancé? Would you have believed her? Yet if they didn't, then her marriage to Joseph would never happen and because she was pregnant outside marriage, Mary could have been stoned to death! That was the punishment in those days for this kind of thing. Yet knowing all the problems she faced in the future, she spoke out and said, "I am blessed."

No matter what we face; whether the future is calm or fraught with danger, let's be like Mary and realise that God loves us, has chosen us and will never leave us!

I AM BLESSED

Praise be to the God and Father
of our Lord Jesus Christ who has
blessed us in the heavenly realms with
every spiritual blessing in Christ.

Ephesians 1:3

I Am Blessed

When I hear you say my name
My fears all melt away
Knowing that you're here with me
And will be everyday
Your Spirit overshadows me
I feel so loved inside
I am your humble servant
My blessings I can't hide

I am blessed
My soul can't stop this rising melody
I am blessed
O so blessed
A living miracle for all to see

How powerful you are, how great
A God of lavish grace
Mercy written in your eyes
For every tribe and race
You lift the weak and hungry ones
Bring rulers to their end
Your favour lasts forever more
On You I can depend

And I sing
Glory, Glory, Glory
Sing
You've done great things for me

> "Learn to love your Bible, God cannot lie!
> He cannot mislead you; He cannot fail!"
>
> James Taylor

This was a message from James Taylor to his young son, Hudson Taylor. Hudson discovered these words to be true throughout his life. He set out as a missionary to China at the age of 21 – alone, without someone to meet him on his arrival, with nowhere to stay and with very little money in his pocket. When he set up the Inland China Mission at a later stage he records that 'all he had was £10 and all the promises of God'. God had called him and he discovered throughout his entire life that God's promises never fail.

Your love O Lord reaches to the heavens, your faithfulness to the skies. Your righteousness is like
the mighty mountains, your justice like the great
deep. O Lord you preserve both man and beast.
How priceless is your unfailing love! Both high and low
among men find refuge in the shadow of your wings.
They feast in the abundance of your house; you
give them drink from your river of delights.
For with you is the fountain of life;
in your light we see light.

Ps 36: 5 – 9

Live in the promises!

More Promises

Matt 28:20

"Surely I am with you always even
to the very end of the age."

Matt 11:28-30

"Come to me, all you who are weary and burdened
and I will give you rest. Take my yoke upon you
and learn from me for I am gentle and humble in
heart and you will find rest for your souls.
For my yoke is easy and my burden is light."

God's promises never fail; each and every one comes to pass.

It's a miracle!

An amazing miracle occurred at my Spiritual Health Weekends in 2010. Many people's lives were affected and I know they will never be the same again.

During 2009 the effects of the recession were being seen all over the land. My Spiritual Health Weekends are usually full many months before the actual conference starts. However, in 2009 we noticed that although the initial response to the weekends was more than ever before, by the autumn when the main bulk of the bookings are received the numbers did not increase vastly. Ray and I went to God in prayer and Ray got a picture of an iceberg blocking the way of a ship and God said that we needed a different ship (a different way) to cut through the ice. We needed a 'ship with an ice cutting edge' to break the ice up. I then brought this to my small team and together we decided to pray more, to fast more and to use a verse of the Bible to focus our attention on God and therefore to cut through the ice. At the same time one of the team said that she thought generosity was also a key.

From the moment we started confessing out our verse of scripture, we saw our own faith and confidence in God rise and also God increased the bookings enormously. I felt God say that I should send an email to everyone on our Spiritual Health Weekend list encouraging them in their own circumstances to believe God for their own financial circumstances whether they were coming to the conference or not. The result was that my inbox was flooded with emails. Some to say, "I really want to come to the weekend but cannot due to financial reasons, but would you please pray for me." Their stories broke my heart as they told us about dire financial circumstances. Others wrote to say that they had joined us in praying and fasting and that since they had done that their faith in God had increased and they were seeing their circumstances change. One lady told us she could not come to the weekend because she had lost her job. But within weeks of praying God had totally changed her situation! She wrote and said, "Nancy, I'm coming, I've booked in." Other ladies wrote and told me that their whole spiritual life in God had increased through concentrating on God and his word rather than on their own circumstances. We had many women up and down our nation praying, fasting and confessing out God's word. It was just amazing! However, I still felt God wanted to do more.

One day whilst praying, God reminded me of the word about generosity and how it was a key to breaking the recession. As I talked with God it became clear that we should pay for some people who were poor to come. I sent out a second email giving an update as to what was happening and mentioned what we felt about generosity. We contacted a few people and had the pleasure of telling them that they could come for nothing. Each one was astonished and cried at the generosity they were being shown. Then something miraculous started to happen. Gifts of £10, £20, £40, £170 came pouring into the office. One lady even sent in £1,000 so that people who were struggling financially could attend. The more places we gave away the more money would come in. On top of this people would contact us to book in their friends telling us that God had told them to pay for their friends to attend. In the end, we received over £3,000 to enable us to issue people with free places. Over 82 people were able to attend through the generosity of others.

Later on in the year when we were preparing for my Spiritual Health Day in Glasgow we again felt God nudge us about being generous. We decided to help not only some of the poor to come but also those who were hurting, abused and marginalised. We contacted various organisations who work with the homeless, the poor, alcoholics and prostitutes and told them that God had said to us to go to the streets and the alleyways and compel them to come to the banquet. Then, I sent an email asking if anyone wanted to join us in helping them to come. Again, we were overwhelmed by people's generosity. This time 70 people were given a free place. God loves it when we invite the poor to his feast! There is much joy in being generous!

**A generous man will himself be blessed,
for he shares his food with the poor.**

Proverbs 22:9

God never calculates how
generous he should be.......
neither should we!

You've stolen my heart

A woman sat in one of my sessions at my Spiritual Health Weekend deeply convicted by God. She had stolen merchandize from the bookshop at my conference which contains mainly my books and CDs. She felt God tell her to return what she had stolen, but the fear of doing so prompted her to ask God to confirm this was really what he wanted her to do. In that particular session I asked people to go through what I called a tunnel of encouragement. This is walking down a line of four to six of my team who have been given verses of scripture from me to read out over the women. When it was this person's turn to walk through the tunnel of encouragement the first verse she heard was Song of Songs 4:9 which says "You have stolen my heart, my sister, my bride; you have stolen my heart!" The moment she heard this, she knew God was speaking to her and she had to confess what had happened and return the stock. Later, she found one of the senior members of my team in the prayer room, gave her the stolen merchandize and explained what she had done. She also explained that since her youth she had a big problem with stealing. Laura prayed with her and thanked her for doing what God had told her to do. What happened next was amazing!

In each session we randomly pick one person out of the hundreds who are there and pray for them as well as give them a special gift which can be flowers, a book, skin products etc. We do this by publicly going through photos of each delegate and counting down from 5 to 1 before saying stop. The person whose photograph is left on the screen, is the one we pick and bless. When we did this at the beginning of the next session, this lady was picked! When I saw what had happened, I was absolutely thrilled! God's grace is totally overwhelming! She had confessed and returned the stock only to find that a few hours later, God choose to highlight her and bless her! The amazing thing was that the gift for that session which was already wrapped to give to whoever was highlighted was a gift of lots of my merchandize from the bookshop! Isn't God wonderful? The lady wrote to us recently to let us know that she has never stolen anything since; her habitual stealing problem has disappeared!

God's grace is totally overwhelming!

Love is patient, love is kind .... it is not easily angered, it keeps no record of wrongs.
Love never fails.

1 Cor 13:4-8

Love

1 John 1:9

He unreservedly accepts us – no matter what we have done!

2 Cor 1:22

He wholeheartedly approves of us and places his seal of ownership on us!

1 John 3:1

He infinitely loves us and calls us his own!

Remember......
**you are special
you are loved**

kind pure wise hospitable cheerful

joyful honouring sincere diligent

peaceful affectionate
forgiving

humble

gentle forgiving

trustworthy upright patient

loving watchful

hopeful

understanding encouraging

BE

truthful generous
thoughtful
comforting
refreshing comforting

special

You!

Do you know?

Laughter

is good for your heart

Kindness

is good for your skin

Forgiveness

is good for your mind

So laugh a lot, spread
kindness around and keep
short accounts by
forgiving

10 Wise Ways

1. Think about positive things. Things of good report. Do not dwell on the negative!

2. Do not worry about anything! Instead pray about everything!

3. Rejoice always; even in the tough times of life look for something or someone to rejoice in.

4. Remember the good things in your life. Write them down; review your list often.

5. Make wise decisions and stick to them

6. Do not let unwholesome words come out of your mouth.

7. Be kind and compassionate always

8. Think of others before yourself.

9. Love God; love yourself; love others.

10. Never forget how special you are

Hope

When I first met the person in this story, I never imagined her story would be so heartbreaking, so complex, yet so amazing at the same time!

Both my parents were alcoholics and had a volatile relationship. They divorced when I was young and I lived with my siblings and my mum. When I was about five or six years old my dad came back to live with us. Both my parents still drank. One night they got into a physical fight with one another and whilst my brother and I were watching, my dad tried to stab my mum to death. My father then stabbed me in my leg! My father went to prison and my mum survived after having over 600 stitches!

We moved into witness protection, changed our names and I thought life was on the up, however, my mum was suffering from severe depression and as a result she committed suicide leaving my brother and me in the care of my uncle. During that time, my uncle subjected me to several different types of abuse. You can imagine how my perception of God was not very good.

I was then put into a children's home, where I lived for two years until I was fostered by a Christian couple. They told me about God, but I didn't want to know! It wasn't until I had a tangible experience of God that I believed in Him.

One night I sat on my bed and I was so depressed I didn't want to live. I was determined to kill myself. I had a bottle of pills in my hand and I said, "If there is a God, you are going to have to show yourself to me, otherwise I am going to die!" At that moment there was a gust of wind in the room and the bottle was knocked to the floor. When I picked up the bottle, the pills had disappeared! I could not understand it. Where had they gone? None of the windows or doors were open, there was no way a gust of wind could have got in to the room and anyway how could pills just disappear, it had to be God!

There and then I gave my life to God, but I was still carrying my past baggage. Not long after this my foster dad, to whom I had become very close, died and because of this the issues of the past were at the foremost of my mind. My foster mum was distraught and four years later she was suffering from depression. All the fears of my biological mum's depression and suicide then came back to haunt me.

A few months previous to this, I had joined New Generation Music. It was there that I began to work through some of the severe issues of my life. God showed me I could not face all these issues in my own strength. He began to strip me of all my burdens and I felt as I wept that all the pain of the past was being dealt with. For the first time ever I accepted and declared God as my loving Heavenly Father. As I put my trust in God as my Father, I discovered his love was nothing like anything I had experienced before. Through knowing his amazing love God dramatically changed me and healed me from the inside out.

Your story might be completely different but God's love for you is just the same. Allow this story to inspire you and bring you hope.

Ambush me with your love

I want to receive as much of your love
as this human heart is able to take

For you created my innermost being, you knit me together in my mother's womb.............My frame was not hidden from you when I was made in the secret place. When I was woven together in the depths of the earth, your eyes saw my unformed body. All the days ordained for me were written in your book before one of them came to be.

Ps 139:13-16

Put your hope in the Lord for with the Lord is unfailing love and with him is full redemption.

Ps 130:7

Joy

Every year at my Spiritual Health Weekends I have a time where I give each delegate a 'word from God'. When a woman books into the conference I take her name into the presence of God and ask him what he would like to say to her. I am often astounded to hear that the words spoken over them are exactly what they need to hear. I am humbled and amazed at how God so often reveals situations that I could not have known.

One day I was praying and bringing one lady's name before God. I started to write a beautiful description of how God saw this lady whose name was Joy. At that point Ray, who was sitting next to me, heard God speak to him. God told him, "The verse you are reading in John 16:24 is for the lady Nancy is praying for right now." Ray read me this verse which talks about joy, totally unaware that the person's name was Joy! When the lady received the word from God she could not believe how accurate it was. She knew the word had to be from God because what neither Ray nor I could have known was that the verse John 16:24 was given to her at birth by her parents and that is why they called her Joy!

Our Father, Abba, knows us by name!

Another Promise

"My beloved and special child, do not fear
when the going gets tough because I will
always be with you! Do not worry when
problems and difficulties seem like a
huge river which threatens to overcome
you, because the river will never wash
you away. When you go through times
that are so tough that you feel like your
existence is being threatened, don't
be concerned because no matter how
hot the fire gets, it will never burn
you! Always remember I am a BIG and
POWERFUL God and I love and adore you!"

Based on Is 43: 1 – 3

You are the Song

You are the song I sing
The music of my life
Every note I hear you play
Takes my fears away
When troubles come around
I tune into your sound
Only you can lift my soul
Up to the heights so beautiful

You are the song I'm singing
Bells are ringing
Hear the oceans roar
Mysterious sound that echoes round
In my head
Across the sky like lightning
You are shining
See the heavens glow
A glorious sight that pierces night
In my soul

You are the only one
Creator of this world
So unforgettable
Supernatural
I see your miracles
Right here before my eyes
That makes me love you all the more
Let the choirs soar

You are the song I'm singing
I hear the bells are ringing
Across the sky you're shining on

What song are you singing?

No place too deep

"There is no place too deep where I cannot find you! There is no problem too huge that I cannot deal with. There is no fear too deeply engrained that I cannot remove! Oh my wonderful and special one, you can fully trust me to deal with every mountain, to flatten every fear and to bring you into a place of great peace and immense joy. You don't have to stay in the dark dungeon anymore, come into the light and live!

Trust me in all your ways! Put me in control and I promise I won't ever fail you!"

Do not be afraid or discouraged, for the Lord God is with you. He will not fail you or forsake you....

1st Chron 28:20

How much are you worth?

"Look at the birds of the air; they do
not sow or reap or store away in
barns and yet your Heavenly Father
feeds them. Are you not much more
valuable than they?"
JESUS

Matthew 6:26

Do you know?

Do you know you are more precious than silver and more valuable than gold? Do you know that I created you in the secret place and formed you in the womb; that I crafted you with love and moulded you with grace? Do you know I chose you to be mine before the world was created? Do you know I made plans for you, plans to prosper you and not to harm you, plans to give you hope and a future?

Do you know?

Do you know that from the beginning I have lovingly carried you in my arms? Do you know that my loving gaze is upon you and that my fragrance is poured over you? Do you know that every day I place my kiss upon your soul and I hug you to myself? Do you know that I have willingly given all for you and I would do it all again!

Do you know? Do you know?

Snowflake

Did you know that physicists tell us that if you looked at all the snowflakes ever made, you would not find any exact duplicates. They explain that each flake is a masterpiece of design but not one design has ever been found to be repeated. Each one is different and yet so special!

If God takes such care and effort for a snowflake which is here for a second and then disappears forever, how much more care, creativity and love does he pour into us! Each one of us is a unique masterpiece of love. Never think of yourself as ugly, useless or worthless for you are an amazing, beautiful, unique, work of art.

**God has given each of us many special gifts;
the gift of love, the gift of joy, the gift
of peace, the gift of grace, the gift
of forgiveness, the gift of life!**

Receive and enjoy each gift!

Each day is brand new....each one created by
a powerful God for you! Each moment is precious and a gift to us; don't spoil even a mil-
lisecond – you can never get it back again!
Live every moment to the full.

John 10:10

Jesus said he was sent to this world to
give us life and life in all its fullness.
ENJOY!

I am standing tall

Though I lose my job and I have no money in the bank, though I have no food on the table and no drinks in the fridge, though I have many bills on my mind and no way of paying them, though the very worst happens and I cannot see the way ahead, yet I will praise my God! I will put my faith and trust in him. I will sing his praises and be joyful despite my circumstances.

The Almighty God is my strength. He enables me to praise even when there is nothing to be joyful about, he enables me to stand tall.

Paraphrase of Habakkuk 3:17-19

Lord give me the grace
to stand tall
Amen

Some people come into our lives
and quickly go. Some stay for awhile
and leave footprints on our hearts
and we are never, ever the same.

Anonymous

Listen, My Special One

"In this world you will have trouble but take heart, I have overcome the world."

John 16:33b

Remember no matter how long or difficult each day can be you never walk alone for God promises to be with you always!

"Never will I leave you; never will I forsake you."

Hebrews 13:5B

The Lord himself goes before you and will be with you; he will never leave you nor forsake you. Do not be afraid; do not be discouraged.

Deuteronomy 31:8

Each moment is like a snowflake, unique, unspoiled, unrepeatable....enjoy each one

Life is unique, precious, beautiful; enjoy every moment, every smile, every peel of laughter, every radiant thought, every passing fragrance, every sign of generosity, every act of kindness, every sign of purity, every encouragement, every gift, every hug, every pleasure, enjoy every good experience – each one has their origin in the Creator!

Come With Me

My lover spoke and said to me, "Arise my darling, my beautiful one, and come with me. See! The winter is past the rains are over and gone. Flowers appear on the earth; the season of singing has come, the cooing of doves is heard in our land. The fig tree forms its early fruit; the blossoming vines spread their fragrance. Arise, come, my darling; my beautiful one, come with me!"

Song of Songs 2: 10-13

Always remember the best is yet to come!

This is Good

As I walked along the beautiful coastline of Scotland, I was reminded of the amazing view I had seen the day before. Ray and I had visited his brother and sister-in-law's new home and had seen the spectacular view of the Firth of Clyde from their balcony. It was stunning! I could have stayed there for ages just taking in the amazing scenery. In the evening when the sun went down, the sky and the sea were filled with amazing colours; pinks, reds and purples. It was incredibly beautiful. I couldn't help thanking God for his amazing creation.

It was then that I remembered that when God created the earth he said 'This is good', but when he created mankind, you and me in all our beauty, creativity and uniqueness, he said,

'This is VERY good!'

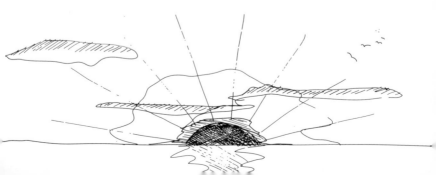

Juliet

A number of years ago when Ray, my husband, visited South Africa he met a beautiful little girl, called Juliet. He didn't realise it at the time, but she had only two weeks to live! Even though Juliet was only 10 years old she had a remarkable story to tell.

A number of years previously, a care worker in South Africa heard that a lady called Primrose was in great distress with deep difficulties and went to see if he could help. He visited the small shack where she lived with her two children to discover a horrific situation. Primrose was HIV positive and her daughter, Juliet, who was also living with the effects of AIDS was extremely ill. Her young son, Themba, was thankfully HIV negative. Primrose had no money or support and had run out of options. The care worker discovered that Primrose had got some rope and was on her way to the nearby railway track to tie herself and her two children to the tracks! She was in despair and could see no way out. The whole family was taken to Sparrow Rainbow Village, the world's first aids village, where they found love, compassion, support and most of all God.

Just shortly after Ray left South Africa, Juliet

called her 'mothers' (her real mum and the carers who had looked after her) to her bed and said goodbye. Little Juliet's brief life was over.

A few weeks later, one of Juliet's carers, Lynette wrote an article for a magazine based on her experience of looking after this special little girl. It was from this article that Ray wrote the song 'For the love of Juliet'.

When Ray first read the lyrics to me, I was busy in my kitchen preparing a meal with lots of issues on my mind. However, as I heard the words of the song, I couldn't stop the tears pouring down my face. Juliet went through some horrendous situations, being turned away from hospitals, being denied the drugs needed to save her life, her mother almost tying her to a railway track but in the end she discovered love and compassion like a never ending stream.

Juliet came to know and understand that she was deeply loved and that she was very special. Do you know you are loved and special? It doesn't matter who you are, because the truth remains firmly in place - you are deeply loved and you are very special and you always will be! Know this truth today and forever!

For the love of Juliet

I can't pretend to understand
All the reasons why
A little girl can be denied
To live instead of die
I feel her gentle eyes on me
Just a quiet look
She's thinking back to special times
Last pages of her book.

Juliet
For the love of Juliet
10 years you walked with tiny feet
Upon this hardened earth
Your footprints hardly left a mark
To say how much, how much you're worth

I begged and even fought with her
To eat to make her strong
We played a game that made her smile
Don't tell me she was wrong
At nine it's time for bath again
She's 14 kilograms

Pretending not to see the signs
I wash her fragile arms

Juliet
For the love of Juliet
10 years you walked with tiny feet
Upon this hardened earth
Your footprints hardly left a mark
To say how much, how much you're worth

The world has washed it's hands of her
There was no love that she could eat
The early hours I cry again
She's going to slip away, away.

She's called her 'mothers' to her bed
She wants to say goodbye
O little sparrow on the ground
Now spread your wings and fly

Loved Beyond All Measure

There is a story in the Bible that talks about a son who despises his father and one day asks for his inheritance. In those days, to ask for your inheritance before your father had died was like saying, "I wish you were dead!" However, even though the son showed no love or respect for his dad, the father loved the son and gave him his inheritance! Once he had his share of the money, he left and went as far away as he could from his childhood home. He splashed his money around on what the Bible calls wild living and had many friends, but when his money ran out so did his so called 'friends'. He was left with nothing! He had no money for food and the only job he could get was looking after pigs! He was so hungry that he wanted to eat what the pigs were eating! It was then that he realised he needed to go home and apologise to his dad and ask him if he could become one of his servants. He knew that even being a servant in his father's home was a huge improvement on his present situation.

Unknown to him, his dad longed for his son to come home and each day he would look to the horizon to see if he could see him returning! One day, the father suddenly spotted him in the distance. His heart began to beat loudly with excitement, his son was coming home! Even though the son had hurt him badly and disgraced him by asking for his inheritance, he ran towards him and when he reached him he engulfed him in his arms. The son did not even get to the end of his well rehearsed speech, before the father had told his servants to organise a banquet to celebrate the son he had missed so badly.

It wasn't in the father's heart to punish his son nor was it to make him realise how deeply he had hurt him. He had forgiven his son a long time ago and although others around him could not understand his actions, he displayed his heart of unconditional love and put it on show for all to see.

Isn't it great to know that we are all loved unconditionally, beyond all measure! Receive the Father's love today!

1 John 3:1

> # How great is the love the Father has lavished on us, that we should be called children of God!

Come Home

After reading the story written by Jacqui Doherty called 'Pete Doherty, My Prodigal Son', my husband Ray wrote the following song. The song reflects the mother heart of God towards any and every prodigal who has walked away from home!

I've watched while you have given love
To dreams that fade away
A self destructive fantasy
That finally makes you pay
'Don't worry, Hey I'll be alright.'
I hear you telling me
But O my child you cannot hear
My tears fall silently

Your dignity like useless waste
Lies rotting in the street
My silent anger screaming out
My child, in so much need
My arms just ache to hold you close
No matter what you've done
My endless hope sings over you
One day, my child, come home

Come Home, Come Home
Where you belong
Can you hear this torn heart?

Come Home, Come Home
I am here waiting
I've been here from the start
I can feel the pain you carry
So please come home
My love, my child, come home

O once again I see you run
Into the fear filled night
Where nothing, no one helps you
Escape your hellish plight
If only you could realise
What treasure's here for you
So come on home just as you are
Into the morning dew

Come Home, Come Home
Where you belong
Can you hear this torn heart?
Come Home, Come Home
I am here waiting
I've been here from the start
I can feel the pain you carry
So please come home
My love, my child, come home

You Are Special

Ray, myself and our two boys were on a special holiday in Florida when tragedy almost struck. When we arrived at our hotel one of the first things we decided to do was to check out the swimming pool. While I locked the car, Ray, Daniel and Aidan went to find loungers around the pool for us to sit on. As I was walking towards them I noticed as Daniel and his dad were organising the chairs Aidan, who was only a toddler, decided he could not wait to go into the pool. I could see what was going to happen. Aidan headed towards the deep end of the pool without waiting for his dad to put on his arm bands. The beautiful swimming pool was just too inviting! I shouted to Ray, but because I was so far away he didn't hear me. Realising that within seconds Aidan was going to be in the pool I panicked and ran towards the pool, throwing my bags and my purse with all our money in it down onto the concrete. However, I was not quick enough to stop Aidan from jumping into the warm water. As I rushed towards the pool, I continued to shout and scream for Ray but he still could not hear me. I arrived at the edge of the pool as Aidan surfaced for the second time. Not stopping for a second, I jumped in fully clothed and got him out safe and sound! As you can imagine it took me some time to calm down! How close we had been to losing Aidan!

It was only afterwards that I realised how strange it must have looked to the others around the pool. As a woman walks by suddenly she starts to shout like crazy and run as though she was being chased by a swarm of bees! As she runs, bit by bit she drops everything she was carrying! I must have looked like a crazed maniac, but this mother did not care at that moment in time about the possibility of looking insane or losing our money and our possessions. My son was more important than my reputation, my belongings or my money! I just wanted to have him safe and sound in my arms.

Just as Aidan and Daniel are very special to us, we are all so incredibly special to God! My love for my boys is only a very small reflection of God's love for each one of us. Never forget that you are deeply loved, incredibly favoured and that you are and will always remain very

Special

Nancy Goudie's
Spiritual Health Weekends

THREE EXCITING DAYS TO TRANSFORM YOUR WALK WITH GOD

Would you like to be pampered physically and toned up spiritually?

Nancy Goudie's Spiritual Health Weekends could be just the thing you are looking for!

Nancy Goudie runs weekend conferences at the end of January and the beginning of February each year at luxury four-star Marriot Hotels in Preston and Bristol. The weekend is for ladies of all ages. Come and enjoy the excellent food and leisure facilities (spa, steam room, sauna, fitness room and luxury pool) and also experience God through the inspirational teaching and creative spiritual exercises from Nancy. Special guests include some of the talented ngm artists. Each conference is booked well in advance so please book early to avoid disappointment.

This is a women's conference like no other!

For more information and booking details contact:

Zoe Wickham at ngm, Caedmon Complex, Bristol Road, Thornbury, Bristol BS35 3JA.

Tel: 01454 414880
Fax: 01454 414812
Email: zoewickham@ngm.org.uk
www.nancygoudie.com

Other Books & Products

By Nancy Goudie

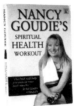

Spiritual Health Workout (£6.99)

This unique book is practical, accessible and fun to use and will help you exercise your faith muscles and tone up your heart for God. It is an excellent book for individuals and small groups.

"The depth of Nancy's faith and spirituality are the genuine products of years of walking with the Lord and seeking to serve him – that's why I am recommending her writing to you" – Steve Chalke, Oasis Trust.

HOT Faith (£7.99)

If you want to find out about how ngm started or the amazing miracles that happened during their five year walk of faith to get their amazing missions and arts centre (Caedmon) then Nancy's book H.O.T. Faith (Hearing, Obeying, Trusting) is the book for you. It is a book filled with stories of faith exploits and will encourage you to walk by faith every day in life.

"Whatever mountains you need to move, this remarkable book will build your faith and empower your prayers"

Pete Greig (24/7 Prayer)

Treasures of Darkness (£5.00)

This is a very naked and honest autobiographical account of a time when the world around Nancy started to collapse. Her husband Ray fell into a dark pit where he experienced ill health and burnout. At the same time God was taking their ministry, ngm, through a shift, which caused much pain and insecurity and led to many people eventually leaving. Pressures swept in like a storm leaving confusion and unanswered prayers. Nancy discovered that through this time there were 'treasures of darkness and riches hidden in a secret place' (Isaiah 45:3).

The Beloved (£5.00 Hardback)

This is a collection of real stories, poems, wise words, meditations and huge encouragement to know that you are God's beloved child. Any time you are feeling down, unloved, criticised or critical of yourself and life hits you hard, then pick up this book and flick through its pages. Each page is designed to bring you words of encouragement, hope and love.

Confident? (£5.00 Hardback)

This book is for anyone who sometimes swings from being confident to feeling a failure. It's a book full of encouragement, wise words, poems, songs and stories to lift your spirit and get you back on your feet again ready to face life once more. Through its pages you will feel accepted, really loved and realise afresh how amazing you are!

Luv Esther (£5.00)

This book takes you behind the scenes of the amazing luv esther musical. It's the story of how luv esther came about; how God provided more than half a million pounds and how God visited ngm with his deep intimacy. It is also a study on the life of Esther which can be used individually or in small groups. *"I throughly recommend this book to you."* – Graham Kendrick

All books are available direct from ngm on **www.ngm.org.uk** or **www.nancygoudie.com** or through Amazon.

Spiritual Health Magazines (£2.00)

Filled with stories, advice, tips and interesting articles – a great glossy magazine to brighten up your day!

Bible Reading Planners (50p)

A superb way of systematically reading through the Bible in one or two years.

Smile (£8.00 Meditation CD)

If you are feeling the daily stresses of life, the busyness of work, the pressures of family or just need some soothing for your soul, then this recording is for you.

Peace Like a River (£8.00 Meditation CD)
If you have ever experienced stress, carried worries, fought fears or are just looking for an oasis in your busy life – then this CD is for you. This recording will take you to a place of tranquillity where peace, love and grace are yours in abundance. Use this CD daily and you will find peace like a river flowing through your soul.

A God Encounter (£5.00 Meditation CD)
A unique meditative worship experience which will transport you to the very throne room of God.

Journey to the Cross (£5.00 Meditation CD)
A powerful CD that will take you to the foot of the cross to experience Christ's death, and impact you with the amazing love of God.

You Are The Song (£9.99 Album CD) *
Hannah's amazing debut album, You Are The Song, is sure to become one of those recordings that is a must in everyone's collection. These songs capture the heart of mercy and are delivered with amazing passion.

All the above books, music and meditation CD's are available direct from ngm, Caedmon Complex, Bristol Road, Thornbury, Bristol. BS35 3JA. Telephone – 01454-414880, www.ngm.org.uk or through www.nancygoudie.com

NANCY GOUDIE CONTACT DETAILS

Should you wish to contact Nancy
then do write to her at:-

ngm,
Caedmon Complex,
Bristol Road,
Thornbury, Bristol. BS35 3JA.

phone – 01454-414880
fax – 01454-414812

nancy@nancygoudie.com
or visit
www.nancygoudie.com.

illustration

<u>contact</u> me if you like:

charlotte@
charlottecookeillustration.com
or
07793239661

www.charlottecookeillustration.com